Whales  and

Other Amazing Animals

by Sharon Franklin

Scott Foresman
is an imprint of

Glenview, Illinois • Boston, Massachusetts • Chandler, Arizona
Upper Saddle River, New Jersey

ISBN 13: 978-0-328-51394-9
ISBN 10:   0-328-51394-6

1 2 3 4 5 6 7 8 9 10 V0G1 13 12 11 10 09

On the Caribbean island of St. Martin, thirty-six pilot whales beached themselves in 2003. Despite efforts to save them, the whales all died.

Along the Massachusetts coast in 2002, more than fifty whales stranded themselves on beaches. Rescuers tried everything they could, but the whales could not be saved.

Whales are beached almost every migration season. Some end up on shore and get stuck in the sand. Others go into a bay and are surrounded by marsh grass. And some swim up narrow channels and get trapped.

Sperm whale

Why do so many whales lose their way? Scientists are not sure, but they have some ideas.

It is hard for whales to see clearly underwater. Because of this, they use clicking sounds to tell where objects are.

Whales make clicking sounds when they blow air through special tubes in their heads. The sounds go out into the water as sound waves. At some point the sound waves bounce off an object and return to the whale in a certain pattern. That pattern tells the whale about the object's shape. This system of "seeing" with sound is called **echolocation**.

Sound waves leave the whale's head, bounce off potential prey, and return to the whale, telling it if there is food ahead.

Some **marine biologists** who study whales think that human activities cause whales to beach. The amount of noise humans produce in the oceans has increased over the years. For instance, sailing ships from the past were quiet. Today, however, large ships are driven by noisy propellers.

It is possible that the noises we make underwater create problems when whales echolocate. Some people also think that **sonar** might disrupt the whales. The navy uses sonar to find submarines.

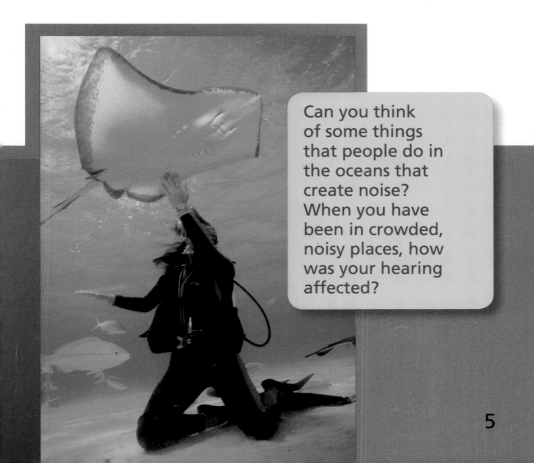

Can you think of some things that people do in the oceans that create noise? When you have been in crowded, noisy places, how was your hearing affected?

Many **species** of whales are endangered. Luckily, there are people who want to help them.

To help whales, we need to understand them better. Scientists around the world are studying how whales behave and communicate. There is no guarantee that we will be able to help all the whales that are endangered. Learning all we can about them will enable us to help them survive.

You can find out how whales behave by going on a whale watch.

The more marine biologists study whales, the more they realize that whales are among the most intelligent animals in the world. For years, marine biologists have been studying whale echolocation and communication. They still don't completely understand how whales use their clicking sounds to communicate with other whales in their pod, or group. One reason that the clicking sounds remain mysterious is that there are many kinds of whales, and each kind uses different sounds and combinations of sounds.

Scientists place special transmitters on some whales in order to study them. The transmitters send a signal to a satellite each time the whales come to the surface. This allows their movements and positions to be tracked.

There are at least seventy species of whales! All the species share some characteristics, but they are different from one another too.

Whales are mammals and have lungs to breathe air. Whales are also known as **cetaceans**. Cetaceans breathe through a blowhole at the back of their heads. The blowhole closes up when they dive to prevent them from drowning.

When whales dive, they use their flippers to steer. The **flukes**, or V-shaped ends of their tails, push them through the water by flapping up and down.

Toothed Whales

Toothed whales have one blowhole. They eat by catching and eating prey with their teeth.

Sperm Whales Up to sixty feet long, they have forty to sixty large teeth in their lower jaw.

Orca Whales Also known as killer whales, they are the fastest mammals in the ocean. Orcas are known to use teamwork to hunt seals.

Narwhal Whales Called the unicorns of the sea, narwhals live in arctic waters. Their horn is actually an unusually long tooth.

Narwhal whale

Whales don't have a sense of smell. They make up for it with their excellent hearing. To stay warm in the cold ocean water, all whales have a thick layer of blubber, or fat.

The chart below compares different types of whales. Orca, narwhal, and sperm whales are toothed whales. Blue, humpback, and right whales are baleen whales.

Blue whale

Baleen Whales

Baleen whales have two blowholes. They eat by filtering small food like shrimp out of the water with plates and brushes that hang down on the inside of their mouths.

Blue Whales Up to one hundred feet long, they are the largest animals on the planet. They are named for their blue color.

Right Whales Up to fifty-eight feet long and very wide, they get their name from the days of whale hunting. They were the "right" whales to catch because they have so much blubber and are slow moving.

Humpback Whales Up to forty feet long, they have especially long flippers that can be one-third of their body length.

Do you know an endangered species that is related to whales? You might guess another marine mammal, such as a manatee. But if you guessed wolves, you could also be right! Scientists think that whales and wolves may both be related to a small, dog-like animal that lived fifty million years ago.

Wolves used to live everywhere in North America. But as people took over the land, they turned wolf habitats into farms, ranches, and cities.

In addition, ranchers began shooting wolves in order to protect their cattle and sheep. Soon there were almost no wolves left in the United States.

Manatee

Scientists were concerned about ecosystems becoming unbalanced without as many wolves. For example, since wolves prey upon elk, the number of elk increased after wolves disappeared. Cottonwood and aspen seedlings are part of the elk's diet. With fewer aspen and cottonwood trees available, beavers had fewer choices of trees to build dams.

Without as many wolves to prey on coyotes, the number of coyotes also increased. Coyotes eat some of the same foods that hawks and eagles eat. Less food for these birds is one of the many reasons they have become endangered.

Scientists felt that they had to do something in order to balance these ecosystems. But how could the balance be restored?

Wolf

In 1995 scientists got the help they were looking for. The federal government ordered biologists to introduce wolves back into the United States. In 1995 and 1996 the biologists brought several dozen wolves to Idaho, Montana, and Wyoming.

To keep track of where the wolves were living, the scientists put special collars on them. The collars had transmitters that sent a signal to a special receiver. This allowed the scientists to know where the wolves were.

Types of Canids

Canids are carnivorous, dog-like animals.

Foxes The fur on most foxes is usually red. Their bodies grow to slightly more than three feet in length. Foxes are solitary. They have learned to adapt to people as we have taken over their habitats.

So far, the plan for returning wolves to the wilderness has been a great success. The original wolves have had pups. Because of the birth of those pups, the number of wolves in the wild is increasing!

Wolf pack

Coyotes Coyotes are about half the size of wolves. They have been seen in cities more and more as humans have pushed them out of their natural habitats. Coyotes are solitary hunters.

Wolves Wolves grow to about three feet at the shoulder. They live in cooperative packs.

Jackals Jackals grow to about two feet at the shoulder. They are scavengers. Jackals are often solitary.

It probably surprised you to hear that whales and wolves may be related. But it should not shock you to hear that wolves and dogs are close cousins.

In fact, dogs are descended from wolves! Scientists are not completely sure how wolves and people first came in contact. They think that wolves might have wandered into the camps of early hunters to find leftover food and bones.

However it happened, at some point people started raising wolf pups. This worked out well because wolves were willing to become part of human society as pets and helpers.

It did not take long for people to understand the benefits of having wolves as pets. Wolves could warn people about dangers by barking. They could also protect people by scaring away other animals that liked to prey on humans.

As time went by, changes occurred to the bodies of these domesticated wolves. Their bodies adapted and evolved into the dogs we know today. People began to rely on them more and more. At first, dogs helped with hunting. Later, farmers trained them to herd sheep and cattle.

Now, dogs are able to do many, many things for us. Can you think of ways people and dogs work together? What about the ways that dogs can help people with physical handicaps?

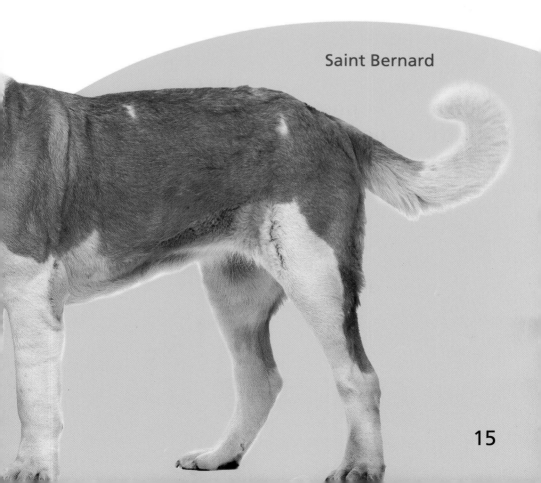

Saint Bernard

Dogs are intelligent and strong, but they cannot live in the human world without help. They cannot buy food at the store. If a dog gets sick, it cannot take itself to the vet. Dogs can only live with people if we help them!

One way that our dogs can get into trouble is by getting lost. After all, they can't ask for directions! That's why it's a good idea to license pet dogs and put name tags on their collars.

New technology can also help find lost dogs. A microchip containing information about a dog's owner can be placed on a dog. If the dog becomes lost, the chip can be scanned to find out how to contact the owner.

A veterinarian places a microchip under a dog's skin.

Dogs, like wolves, are members of the canid family. How many of the dogs in the chart do you recognize?

Types of Dogs

Type	Description	Popular Examples
Sporting	The dogs in this group are good at helping their owners hunt in water or in the woods.	golden retriever, Labrador retriever, cocker spaniel
Hound	Dogs in this group are the best at tracking things by their smell.	bloodhound, basset hound, beagle
Herding	These dogs can get other animals to move where they want them to go and often try to "herd" their owners.	Australian shepherd, border collie, German shepherd

German shepherd and golden retriever

Dogs are popular pets. But people keep many other pets besides dogs. Fish, rabbits, horses, gerbils, and cats also make good pets. Would it surprise you to learn that some animals like cats as pets too?

The famous gorilla Koko, who was raised by animal psychologist Penny Patterson, has had three pet cats. She named them All Ball, Lipstick, and Smokey. Koko and Penny live near each other. Every day, Penny teaches Koko how to communicate using American Sign Language.

Adult and young gorilla

Koko can understand many of the things people say. She can also use her hands to "speak" sign language and tell people what she thinks or wants.

Washoe, a chimpanzee, also communicates with sign language. Her adopted baby chimp has learned to use sign language too.

Gorillas and chimps belong to the primate family. A **primate** is a kind of land mammal with a large brain and flexible fingers and toes. Gorillas and chimps can communicate with each other using sounds and gestures. And chimpanzees are able to make and use simple tools in the wild.

Sadly, apes are now endangered. Their forests habitats have been cut down. Chimpanzees and gorillas are hunted for food. Young gorillas and chimpanzees have been stolen from their mothers and sold illegally as pets.

Chimpanzee

19

Rwanda

Borneo

ASIA

AFRICA

Tanzania

Types of Apes

Chimpanzees
Chimpanzees live in troops of up to eighty. They live in the trees and on the ground. Chimps eat mainly fruit, leaves, buds, insects, and small animals. An adult male chimp weighs about 110 pounds and measures a little more than four feet tall.

Gorillas
Gorillas live in groups of thirty or fewer members. They spend most of their time on the ground. Gorillas are vegetarians, eating bamboo, celery, and fruit. An adult male might weigh almost five hundred pounds and can grow to nearly six feet tall.

Fortunately, scientists around the world are working to save apes. For decades Jane Goodall observed generations of chimp families living in Tanzanian forests. Her observations have helped people understand chimps better and have given us new ways to help apes survive.

In Rwanda, Dian Fossey observed the gorillas of the African rain forest. People have been able to help gorillas much more because of Fossey's work.

In Borneo a Dutch woman named Biruté Galdikas has an orangutan rehabilitation center. At the center, Galdikas teaches orangutans how to live in the wild again. Because of Galdikas's work, many more orangutans are now living free in their natural habitat.

Bonobos Bonobos are closely related and similar in size to chimps. They weigh up to about 130 pounds and grow to about four feet tall. Fruit is the favorite food of bonobos. They also eat small animals, as well as shoots and leaves.

Orangutans With their strong arms, orangutans are able to swing through the trees. They eat fruit and leaves. An adult male weighs about two hundred pounds. He grows to about 4 ½ feet tall.

Now Try This

At your home, school, or town library, type the words *Endangered Species Program* into a search engine on a computer. Search for sites relating to the United States Fish and Wildlife Service. These sites usually have *.gov* at the ends of their Web addresses.

Once you locate a site, read to find information on the endangered and threatened species that are found in your state. Think about the animals that interest you and choose one that you would like to help. Then research the animal using encyclopedias, library books, and the Internet.

Here are some questions for you to answer as you research your animal.

- Is it considered threatened or endangered?

- How many are left in your state?

- Where in your state is the animal found?

- What is the greatest problem facing the animal?

- What can you do to help the animal?

In small groups, present what you and your classmates have found out. You will learn about the animal you chose as well as many others!

Glossary

canids *n.* carnivorous, dog-like animals.

cetaceans *n.* marine mammals that breathe through a blowhole. Whales, dolphins, and porpoises are cetaceans.

echolocation *n.* a process for locating objects by sending out sound waves and listening for their echo.

flukes *n.* the two halves of a whale's tail that help it to swim.

marine biologists *n.* scientists who study the plants and animals of the ocean.

primate *n.* a group of mammals that includes apes and monkeys. Primates are among the most intelligent animals on Earth.

sonar *n.* a method for detecting objects, especially underwater, with sound waves.

species *n.* a set of related living things that share certain characteristics.